How to p

HOCKEY

a step-by-step guide

Text:
Liz French

Technical consultant:
Steve Bowling

JARROLD

Other titles in this series are:

AMERICAN FOOTBALL	**CROQUET**	**SQUASH**
BADMINTON	**DINGHY SAILING**	**SWIMMING**
BOWLS	**GET FIT FOR SPORT**	**TABLE TENNIS**
BASKETBALL	**GOLF**	**TENNIS**
COARSE FISHING	**SNOOKER**	**WINDSURFING**
CRICKET	**SOCCER**	

How to play HOCKEY
ISBN 0-7117-0490-2
First published in Great Britain, 1991
Text copyright © Liz French, 1991
This edition copyright © 1991 Jarrold Publishing
Illustrations by Malcolm Ryan

Designed and produced by
Parke Sutton Limited, Norwich
for Jarrold Publishing, Norwich

Contents

Introduction

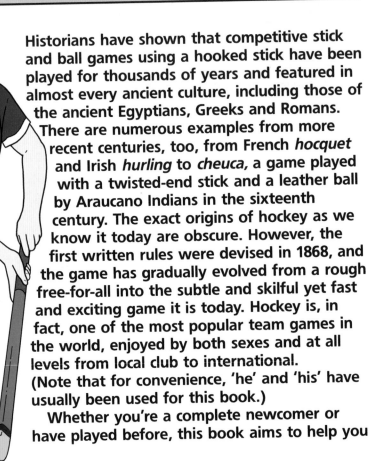

Historians have shown that competitive stick and ball games using a hooked stick have been played for thousands of years and featured in almost every ancient culture, including those of the ancient Egyptians, Greeks and Romans. There are numerous examples from more recent centuries, too, from French *hocquet* and Irish *hurling* to *cheuca,* a game played with a twisted-end stick and a leather ball by Araucano Indians in the sixteenth century. The exact origins of hockey as we know it today are obscure. However, the first written rules were devised in 1868, and the game has gradually evolved from a rough free-for-all into the subtle and skilful yet fast and exciting game it is today. Hockey is, in fact, one of the most popular team games in the world, enjoyed by both sexes and at all levels from local club to international.
(Note that for convenience, 'he' and 'his' have usually been used for this book.)
Whether you're a complete newcomer or have played before, this book aims to help you

get the most from your game. As well as a clear explanation of the game itself, you'll find practical tips on, for example, the type of stick to choose and what shoes to wear, as well as step-by-step instructions on the various techniques and some suggestions for practising on your own.

Of course, no book is a substitute for actually playing! If you want to get started in hockey, you'll find most clubs welcome keen newcomers. Ask at your local sports centre or library for details of clubs in your area; most will have a coaching scheme. Joining a club is a great way to make new friends as well as to enjoy the game, for hockey teams are invariably friendly and lively. If you have trouble finding a club, you can contact The Hockey Association at 16 Northdown Street London N1 9BG (tel: 071 837 8878) or the All England Women's Hockey Association, 3rd Floor, Argyle House, 29-31 Euston Road, London NW1 2SD.

Note: Indoor hockey is a variation not covered in this book since it is in many ways a very different sport. It is popular with many players as a means of developing and improving their skills.

PITCH AND EQUIPMENT

The Pitch

The standard hockey pitch is rectangular, 100 yds (91.4 m) long and 60 yds (55 m) wide with clearly marked boundaries and markings as shown here. Flagposts are placed at each corner and at the halfway (centre) line. The surface can be either natural or synthetic grass; 'all-weather' pitches are increasing in number.

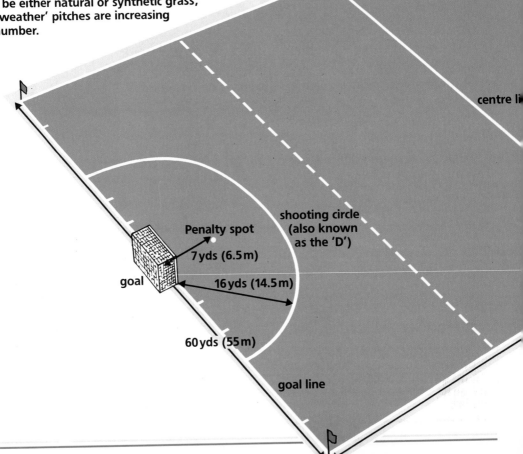

centre line

shooting circle (also known as the 'D')

Penalty spot

7 yds (6.5 m)

goal

16 yds (14.5 m)

60 yds (55 m)

goal line

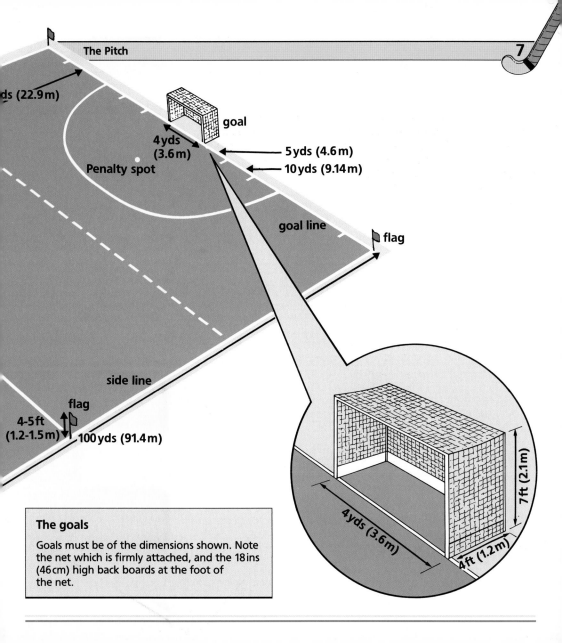

ds (22.9m)

goal

4 yds
(3.6m)

5 yds (4.6 m)

10 yds (9.14 m)

Penalty spot

goal line

flag

side line

flag

4-5 ft
(1.2-1.5 m)

100 yds (91.4 m)

7 ft (2.1 m)

4 yds (3.6 m)

4 ft (1.2 m)

The goals

Goals must be of the dimensions shown. Note
the net which is firmly attached, and the 18 ins
(46 cm) high back boards at the foot of
the net.

Equipment

The ball

The ball is similar to a cricket ball, except that it is usually white. It must weigh between 5½ oz (156 gm) and 5¾ oz (163 gm) but can be hollow or solid. The outer surface can be made of any material — the traditional ball is of leather but plastic is common. The surface can be smooth or dimpled. The dimensions are important and are shown here.

Circumference:
8¹³/₁₆ ins (22.4 cm) - 9¼ ins (23.5 cm)

Before some matches umpires may check that your stick passes through a 2 in (5.1 cm) diameter ring.

The stick

The head of the stick — the part at the bottom under the 'splice' — is curved and made of mulberry, an exceptionally hard wood. It must be no longer than 4 ins (10 cm), with no sharp edges. The head must be flat on one side — this is its 'face'. The handle is made of cane reinforced with rubber and wood.
Sticks can vary in weight between 12 oz (340 gm) and 28 oz (793 gm)

Hint box: choosing and looking after a stick

● Don't buy your own stick until you've played for a while and know what weight suits you best.

● Buy from a reputable sports shop.

● Try the 'feel' of many different sticks to find one with a balance, weight and length which suits you.

● Don't choose one that's too heavy — about 19 or 20 oz (538 or 566 gm) is an average.

● Look down the stick's length and check that the grain follows the curve of the blade.

● Clean your stick after every game.

● Rub a little oil into the head occasionally with a soft cloth.

Dress

The hockey kit is fairly simple and traditional, consisting of shorts and shirt for men, skirts for women.

Players in a team all wear the same colour shirt, except for the goalkeeper who must wear a different colour. Shirts are numbered to identify players (see page 11). Shorts and socks are also identical for all team members.

Protective clothing

All players wear shin and ankle pads. Protecting your hands and knuckles with tape is also highly recommended, as is using a gum shield. Helmets incorporating face masks are compulsory for goalkeepers (see page 38).

Footwear

Your footwear's main function is to give a good grip on the ground. But what you wear depends on which surface you're playing on.

● For natural grass, boots with moulded nylon or screw-in rubber studs are best — most people wear football boots.

● For artificial grass, nylon multi-studded boots are most suitable.

● For other synthetic surfaces (eg rubber), training shoes are better.

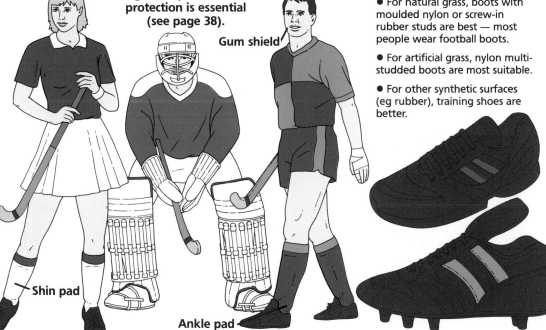

For goalkeepers, all-round protection is essential (see page 38).

Gum shield

Shin pad

Ankle pad

THE GAME

Hockey is played between two teams of eleven players, both trying to gain and keep possession of the ball and score goals by propelling the ball into their opponents' goal.

The Umpires

The game is controlled by two umpires who administer the rules. Each takes one diagonal half of the ground for the whole game and they operate on opposite sidelines. They normally only make decisions for their own half of the field. The umpires have wide discretionary powers and their basic functions are:

- To start the game.
- To judge fair and unfair play.
- To stop play as necessary when an infringement occurs.
- To issue penalties and warnings as necessary (see pages 14-19).
- To act as timekeepers.

The umpires use a variety of hand signals to indicate decisions. Most of these are self-explanatory (eg pointing towards the corner indicates that a long corner has been given). Here are some of the less obvious ones.

Penalty corner
(point towards goal)

16-yard hit

Penalty stroke

Goal (point towards centre spot)

The Players

Players within a squad (including substitutes) are numbered from 1-16, usually for identification only rather than to indicate their positions on the field. Actual formations or 'systems' vary — see page 43.

Players adopt different positions known by specific names depending on the system of play. The divisions of responsibility are not entirely rigid, however. Team members work together within the adopted system, co-operating with every other team member either directly or indirectly. But there are some very broad areas of responsibility as shown on the table below.

	Basic role	Positions	Skills/Attributes
Forwards	Almost wholly attacking	Right wing/left wing Centre forward/striker Outside right/left	Shooting Speed Passing
Midfielders	Create and support attacks Mark opposing midfielders Support defenders	Right half/left half Centre half Centre midfield Inside left/inside right Left midfield/right midfield	Marking Passing Shooting Stamina
Defenders	Primarily defensive	Sweeper Full back (left back/right back) Centre back	Ability to 'read' the game Marking Tackling Passing

Substitutes

In addition to the eleven players it has on the field at the start, each team is allowed to make three substitutions at any time during a game — though not to replace a team member who has been sent off for misconduct (see page 15).

Playing the Game

Duration

A game is usually played over two 35-minute periods, with a half-time interval of 5-10 minutes. At the end of each half, the umpires will add any time lost through stoppages or injuries.

Starting

The two captains toss a coin before the game starts. The winner can choose: to have possession of the ball at the start of the game **OR** which end to attack in the first half.
The other captain automatically has the second option.

Pass/push back

At the start of play, whichever team has possession plays a pass back from the centre of the field. Usually the centre-forward takes the pass back.
All players must be in their own half of the field.
All players in the opposing team must be at least 5 yds (4.5 m) away from the ball.
The ball may be hit or pushed along the ground but not intentionally raised.
The ball is considered to be in play once it has been moved from its original starting point.
A pass back is also played after a goal has been scored.

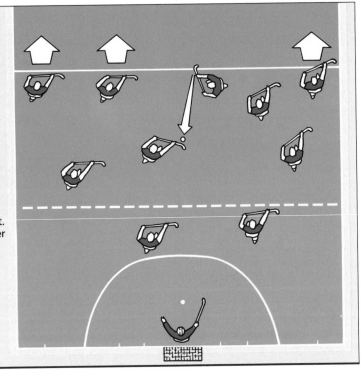

The aim of the game

The basic idea, of course, is to get and keep possession of the ball and propel it towards — and into — your opponents' goal, while preventing the other team from doing the same. The techniques for doing this will be found later in the book, but first you should know what you can and cannot do.

Get the rule book!

There are eighteen main rules in hockey, designed to cover all eventualities. If you're serious about the game, it is worth getting a copy of the official Rule Book, available from the Hockey Association or All England Women's Hockey Association — addresses on page 5.

Goals

For a goal to count, the ball must pass completely over the goal line, under the crossbar and between the goal posts. It must have been hit or deflected by an attacker who was within the shooting circle at the time.

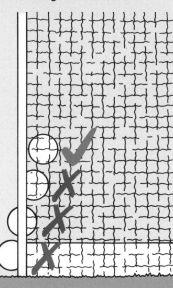

National umpires kit

When The Ball Goes Out

What happens when the ball leaves the field depends on where and when this occurs.

Long corner

A corner is taken if the ball is unintentionally sent behind the goal line by a defender from less than 25 yds (22.9 m) from the goal line.

● The corner is taken by an attacker.

● The ball is placed on the goal line within 5 yds (4.5 m) of the corner flag.

● All opposing players must stand at least 5 yds (4.5 m) away from the ball.

16-yard hit

This is awarded to the defending side if the ball is played over the goal line by an attacking player — very similar to a goal kick in soccer.

● The hit is taken from a spot in line with the point where the ball went over the goalline, and no more than 16 yds (14.5 m) away from that line.

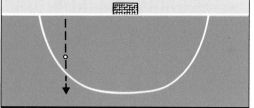

Push-in/hit-in

This is used when the ball passes completely over one of the side lines.

● It is taken by a member of the team opposing the player who last touched the ball.

● The ball is placed on the line at the spot where it went out.

● All the opposing players must be at least 5 yds (4.5 m) away from the ball.

Hint box: taking push-ins/ hit-ins and long corners

● All other team members should move to create space and passing opportunities.

● You have unopposed possession of the ball — don't waste it.

● Take the ball as quickly as you can without losing possession.

● As you approach the ball, look to see where your team-mates are — who is unmarked?

● A corner should result in a goal attempt.

● Practise set moves with your team and use signals to indicate your plans.

When An Infringement Occurs . . .

Hockey is a fast, furious and physical game and infringements of the rules inevitably occur. See the following pages for the most common. The penalty for an infringement depends on where and when it occurs. Most infringements are penalised with a free hit to the other side. A breach by a defender in the circle results in a penalty corner or penalty stroke. For serious offences, the umpire can also give a warning, by showing a player a green card. Temporary suspension from the game is indicated with a yellow card and permanent disqualification for the rest of the game by a red card.

Free hit

● This is taken from the spot where the offence occurred.

● The striker may push or hit it but not intentionally raise it.

● Players from the opposing side must be at least 5 yds (4.5 m) away from the ball.

● If a free hit to an attacking side is within 5 yds (4.5 m) of the defenders' circle, players of both sides must be 5 yds (4.5 m) from the ball.

● The player taking the free hit must not touch the ball again or stay within playing distance of it until another player has touched it.

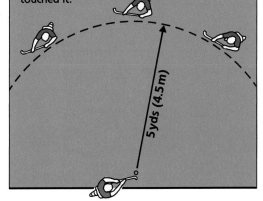

5 yds (4.5 m)

Penalty corner

● Awarded when an offence is committed by the defending team in their own defensive circle or, sometimes, within their own 25 yds (22.9 m) area.

● Taken from a point on the goal line at least 10 yds (9 m) from the nearest goal post.

● No attacker is allowed in the circle until the ball has been hit or pushed.

● No more than five defenders are allowed behind the goal line as the corner is taken — the others must be beyond the halfway line.

● No defender may cross the goal line, and no attacker may enter the circle, until the ball has been played.

● You can't score direct from a penalty corner — the ball must be stopped by another player. before a shot can be made.

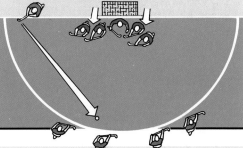

Penalty stroke

This is just like a penalty in soccer, awarded after an offence by the defenders in their circle which may affect the outcome of the game — ie stop the attackers from scoring.

- Taken from the 7 yds (6.5 m) spot.

- The goalkeeper must not move his feet until the stroke is taken.

- All other players must stay beyond the nearer 25 yds (22.9 m) line until the stroke is taken.

- Unlike a goal attempt during open play, play does not continue after the stroke — a goal or 16-yard hit are the only possible outcomes. No rebound attempts are allowed.

The bully

This was formerly used to start and restart play but is now only used after a simultaneous breach of the rules by both teams, or after accident or injury.

- Two players, one from each team, stand opposite each other. Each player faces one side line and has his own goal line to his right.

- The ball is placed on the ground between them.

- The two players must tap their sticks alternately on the ground and together three times before the ball can be played. Each then tries to win the ball.

- All other players must be at least 5 yds (4.5 m) away from the ball until it is in play.

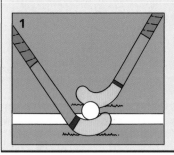

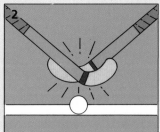

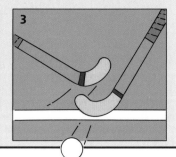

Offences

Note: Some of these do not apply to the goalkeeper — see pages 38-39.

1 Off-side

As in other team field games, an off-side rule is needed to stop attackers from hanging around near the goal waiting for the ball to be passed to them. It's a rule which sometimes leads to confusion. Put simply, you will be given off-side if:

● You are ahead of the ball in the opposing 25 yds (22.9 m) area
AND
● There are fewer than two opponents (one of whom is usually the goalkeeper) between you and the back-line **at the moment the ball is played.**
You'll only be penalised for being off-side if the umpire considers that you've interfered with play or impeded an opponent, or gained some advantage from your position.

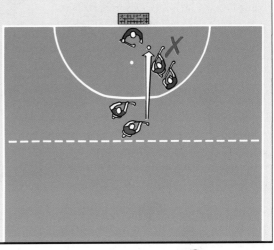

2

Playing the ball with the rounded side of your stick. Only the flat side of the stick may be used.

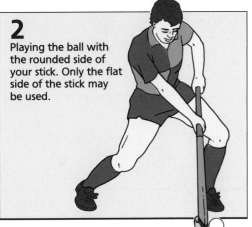

3

Taking part in, or interfering with, the game without having your own stick in your hands.

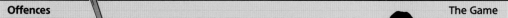

4

Raising your stick in a threatening or dangerous way, especially when stopping, playing or attempting to play the ball.

5

Playing the ball dangerously or in a way likely to lead to danger.

6

Stopping or propelling the ball either in the air or on the ground with any part of your body including your hand.

7

Using your leg or foot to support the stick so as to resist an opponent.

8

Kicking, picking up or carrying the ball.

9

Hitting at, hooking, holding or otherwise interfering with an opponent's stick.

10

Charging, kicking, striking or holding an opponent.

11

Obstructing or stopping an opponent playing the ball by interposing your body or stick between your opponent and the ball.

Grip

For good control of the stick, you need a sound grip. This will vary a little for different strokes and actions, but here is the basic, conventional grip to use when dribbling (see opposite).

Spread the thumb and forefinger of both hands to make 'V' shapes. Hold the stick with your left hand near the upper end and your right hand about 6-12 ins (15-30 cm) lower down, with the 'V' shapes pointing straight down the stick. Your left hand is responsible for twisting and rotating it, whilst the right hand gives stability and control.

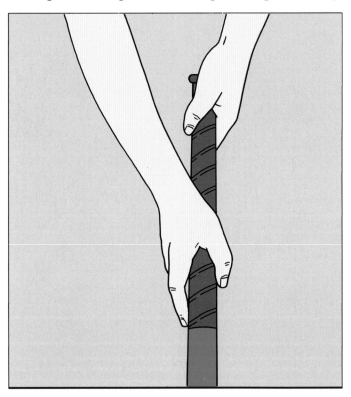

Hint box: stick control

If you're new to the game, it's worth spending time just getting the feel of moving and controlling the stick, without even using a ball.

● Rotate the stick, concentrating on co-ordinating your wrist action.

● Remember, your left hand controls the movement.

● Your right hand lets the stick move within it, grasping it firmly again as you complete the movement.
This is an open-stick side rotated anti-clockwise — a reverse stick.

Dribbling

Dribbling, or running with the ball under close control, is a basic skill and not hard to master. It is a useful and effective way of getting out of trouble in defence, and of creating goal-scoring chances. But be warned — there is also a strong risk of losing possession to an opponent. If you have a choice, passing (see page 22) is a safer option.

Here we describe an Indian dribble, in which the ball is tapped or dragged repeatedly from left to right, using twisting movements of the wrists. You can also dribble in a straight line with either an open or reverse stick.

1

First try patting the ball from side to side while you're standing still. The ball should go straight out at right angles to your body. As you tap the ball to the left, the stick is open-sided.

2

To knock the ball to the right you use a reverse stick.

3

Now progress to moving with the ball, first walking and then gradually building up speed. The ball should be aimed at an angle so you've always got it under control. Note the bent knees and slight crouching of the body.

Passing

Hockey is a team game and effective passing from one team member to another is essential to success. There are a number of different strokes that can be used to get the ball from one player to another. First, a few general points to consider.

Scanning

This simply means knowing what's going on around the field and acting accordingly. It entails lifting your head quickly and taking in as complete a picture as possible. It's a vital skill whatever you're doing in the game but particularly important if you're about to make a pass. It's no good receiving the ball and getting control of it if you don't know what your team-mates and opponents are doing. So get into the habit of scanning and anticipating — you'll make yourself a more useful team member.

Timing

When passing, remember that the player you are passing to will probably be moving — so aim at the spot which he will be at when he receives your pass. If you are the receiving player, concentrate on anticipating where the ball is going to be and getting yourself into position to receive it.

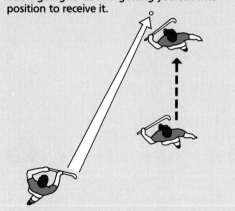

Hint box: passing

● During a game, constantly ask yourself, 'What would I do with the ball if I had it now?'
● Always be aware of where your team-mates are.
● When you have made a pass — **move** to a position where you can take a return pass.

The Push

The push is a stroke which drives the ball along the ground. It is arguably the most important stroke in the game, giving accuracy and speed over both long and short distances. It can be used for shooting at goal (see page 36) as well as passing.

Grip

Hold the stick firmly with your left hand at the top of the stick and your right hand halfway down (moving your right hand down gives you more control).

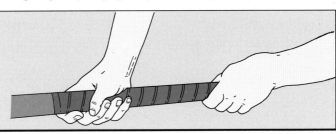

Action

Your left foot and shoulder point towards your target. Crouch over with your knees bent and keep your head well down over the ball.
Now literally push the ball along the ground, keeping your stick in contact with the ball for as long as possible. Angle the face of your stick downwards to stop the ball rising. Complete the stroke with your stick pointing in the direction the ball has gone. The power for the stroke depends on the speed at which the stick head strikes the ball.

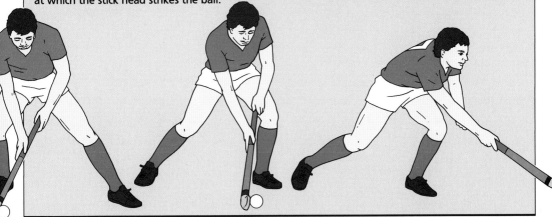

The Reverse Stick Pass

If you have time, it's usually best to use an open-stick stroke. But you will sometimes need to pass with the reverse stick — and this can also be a usefully deceptive stroke, to hide a short left-to-right pass.

Grip

As for a push pass. Keep a good firm grip with your hands comfortably apart.

Action

Practise making the pass off either foot and without slowing down your run.
The ball is close to your right foot as you strike it with the toe of your stick.
Again, keep the stick in contact with the ball for as long as possible.

The Hit

This is used for speed and power over longer distances, including crosses into the circle and shots at goal. Its main drawback is the time it takes to set up the shot — although only a split second — makes it hard to disguise. Practise hitting while standing still and on the run.

Grip

Position your hands close together near the top of the stick. Keep a firm grip to avoid twisting the stick as it contacts the ball: this would cause the ball to deviate. (It is possible to use a deliberate twist of the wrists to impart spin, but this is an advanced technique.)

Action

Your left shoulder points towards your target. Start with your weight on your back foot and swing the stick behind your right shoulder. Weight is transferred onto your left foot for power as you sweep the stick forward through the ball as fast as you can. Keep your eyes on the ball until after you've hit it, and follow through the stroke. Ideally, the ball should be level with your left foot as you make contact. In practice you may have to strike it nearer your right foot.

The Slap

Another common technique, this is almost a cross between a push and a hit. It is an effective stroke over longer distances, and powerful despite a relatively short backswing. It is also quite easily disguised.

Grip

As for a push pass, with the right hand well down for good control.

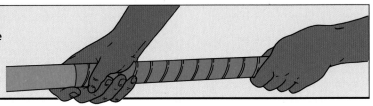

Action

Approach the shot as if for a push, but on the downward swing transfer your weight from the back to the front foot. As you make contact with the ball, bring your left hand quickly back towards your body and accelerate your right hand through the ball in a sweeping or levering action.

The Flick

This is a sort of overhead push used to lift the ball over the opposition. The idea is to get the stick under the ball and keep it in contact for as long as you can. The flick can be executed while you are standing still or running, the latter being much more difficult.

Grip

Have your hands apart on the stick as if for a push.

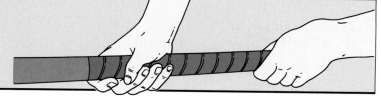

Action

As for a push, bend low on your right foot, with your head well over the ball and your left shoulder facing the target. The point of contact is with the ball well ahead of the left foot.
Position the stick underneath the ball with the face angled upwards.
Your weight is transferred onto your front foot to generate power as you execute the stroke.
Concentrate on trying to lift the ball upwards and forwards.

Receiving The Ball

Gathering the ball and getting it quickly under control ready for the next move is just as vital as accurate passing. You need to be able to perform the whole sequence quickly and

1 On the ground

Hold the stick in the usual way, hands apart. Keep your weight well forward by bending your knees and body. Get head and body in line with the path of the ball.

Pull back your lower hand so the stick is angled downwards. Let your right hand relax at the moment of impact to minimise rebound.

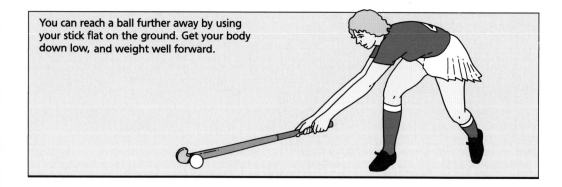

You can reach a ball further away by using your stick flat on the ground. Get your body down low, and weight well forward.

smoothly, whether the ball is coming at you from the front or from the side, along the ground or in the air. Practise them all with both open-stick and reverse-stick side.

2 In the Air

A. Remember that you mustn't play the ball unless it is at shoulder height or lower. Grip, head and body position are as before. Keep your stick below shoulder level and get in line with the ball.

B. Angle the stick so as to deflect the ball downwards, bringing it under control near your feet.
Keep your eyes on the ball all the time.
As before, let your lower hand 'give' to absorb the impact.

C. Trapping a ball in the air on the reverse-stick side.

Running

Running is an important part of hockey — in fact, you can easily run several miles during a match. So you need to be fit and agile, able to run well, and especially to stop, start and change direction quickly and smoothly. You can practise this at any time, of course, without a ball or stick — see some further suggestions on pages 46-47.

Running with the ball

This can mean dribbling (see page 21) or moving the ball into open space.
For the latter:

● Your grip is slightly modified, with the right hand higher up the stick than usual.

● Your stance should be as upright as possible.

● If you see an empty space, move into it.

● Keep the stick and ball ahead of you and to the right so that you can keep up your speed.

● Remember to keep scanning (see page 22) as you run so that you are always ready for the next move.

Running without the ball

This is important too, especially when you realise that in an average game, you'll only have possession of the ball for about three minutes! The rest of the time you should:

● Watch the ball.

● Keep moving.

● Look for space and move into it to give the player with the ball passing options.

● In defence, watch for chances to gain possession.

● When you get the ball, use it well, then start again.

Getting Past An Opponent

If an opponent is waiting to tackle, the best way to beat him is by passing the ball to a team-mate. If this is not possible, you have to take the ball past him, either on his open (right) side or reverse (left) side. To succeed, you must deceive your opponent by dodging and *feinting* so that he is wrong-footed for the split-second you need to get past. Speed, balance and timing are all vital here.

If you want to pass on your opponent's right, step firmly onto your right foot. This should fool the defender into moving left. Then push off powerfully onto your left foot and move the ball past the defender on his open side.

For passing on the defender's left, your first step is on your left foot. Wait for your opponent to commit himself in that direction.
Then off you go on your opponent's reverse side. Sounds simple, but in practice you'll need to dodge and feint rather more than this suggests if you are to beat opponents successfully!

Hint box: successful dodging

● Approaching the defender at about half your maximum speed gives you better control than racing along at top speed.
● Keep the ball close to your stick all the time to avoid having it stolen.
● The moment to move comes when you catch your opponent off-balance — but you must act quickly to make use of this split-second advantage.

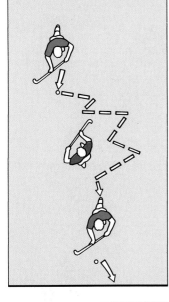

Defending

When your team loses possession of the ball you must all work together to win it back. The easiest way is to intercept a pass made from one opponent to another, but marking and tackling are important defence skills too.

Marking

Marking means keeping close to an opponent to make it hard for him to receive a pass or get away from you. It needs fast footwork and balance — and lots of practice.

● Mark one opponent.

● How close you get depends on where the ball is — the greater the chance of a pass coming to your opponent, the closer you should be.

● Always try to get between your goal and your attacker.

● Concentrate on your opponent first and foremost, then on the ball — but don't lose sight of the overall situation.

● Always ask yourself: 'What would I do with the ball if I got it now?'

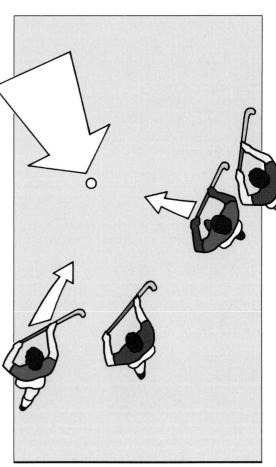

Tackling

Tackling means using your stick to win the ball if you can, but if not , to weaken the attacker's control over it or to send the ball out of play. There are three main types of tackle: jab, open-side and reverse-side.

Hint box: tackling

- Watch the ball carefully and don't be taken in by *feints*.
- Look to see what passing options your opponent has, and try to move so you cut down his chances.
- Use stick and body *feints* of your own to force an error.
- Keep the head of your stick near the ground.
- An attacker will usually move the ball away from a defender's stick — think carefully about where you position your stick so you influence his movements.

Jab tackle

This needs speed and balance. The idea is to get your stick under the ball and jab it away from the attacker .

- Close down the gap between you and the attacker, holding your stick in both hands.

- Feint some dummy tackles to try to throw your opponent off balance.

- As soon as you succeed, stab at the ball with the stick, holding it in your left hand and bringing your left foot forward.

- Be careful not to over-balance — you'll need enough control to tackle again if you don't get the ball away first time.

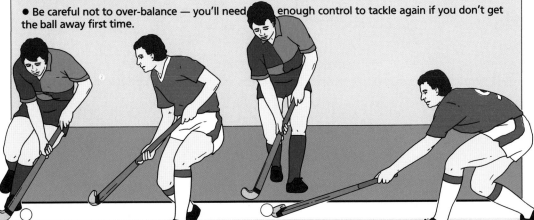

Open-side tackle

This is the most commonly used tackle and is sometimes known as a block tackle. It is generally used if your opponent is committed to getting past you on your right. It can be performed whilst stationary or on the move, and from a variety of angles. Timing and balance are again, vital factors in your success.

- If you're on the move, try to get alongside your opponent, between him and the goal, before you tackle.

- Grasp the stick firmly with your right hand well down.

- Lead with your left foot.

- As soon as your opponent shows any loss of control or balance, get your stick on the ball.

Reverse-side tackle

This is more difficult, but important to master for when you need to tackle an opponent on your left side. The aim is to trap the ball so the attacker over-runs it, then get the ball away and set up an attacking chance for your own team. It is usually a one-handed movement, so you need a fairly strong left arm and wrist as well as good timing and balance. You need to be level with, or ahead of, your opponent to execute the tackle cleanly.

● Keep your body position low.

● Use two hands if at all possible — but usually you will only be using your left hand.

● Twist your wrist fully in an anti-clockwise direction as you reach out for the ball.

● Keep the head of the stick pointing downwards and hook the stick over the ball, then drag it away from the attacker.

● Remember that you must not contact your opponent's stick or body — be very careful or you could give the other side a free hit.

If you're tackling from further away you'll need to lay down your stick, presenting it horizontally to trap the ball against the ground as in a reverse stick trap.

Shooting

Hockey is basically all about goal scoring, and understanding good shooting practice is vital. So here is the basic how, when and where of shooting.

How?

Ideally, of course, you'd find yourself in the 'D' with the ball perfectly placed and plenty of time to choose the spot and prepare the shot. But hockey's not like that! In fact, goal scoring is as much about improvisation and maximising any chances as it is about preparation. Not all players have a natural scoring instinct and ability, but practice, practice and more practice will certainly help you develop good shooting skills.

● When you get the ball within the circle, scan quickly to assess the positions of the defence, the goalkeeper and the goal itself.

● Decide the direction and force of your stroke.

● Get into the best body position you can without losing time.

● Keep your eyes on the ball and **shoot!**

● Use whatever stroke is appropriate. The slap (see page 26) is very useful because it gives you accuracy and speed.

● A shortened grip is often effective, with the top hand brought down to the lower hand to give more wrist action.

Hint box: rebounds

Remember that, unlike in soccer, the goalkeeper cannot catch and hold the ball. A shot that is saved is very likely to rebound offering another chance to score. If you're playing in a forward position, learn to watch for and anticipate the possibilities.

When?

Do shoot:

● Whenever you are within the shooting circle and have a chance, or even half a chance.

● Quickly — you need a balance between using your instincts and weighing up the possibilities. Delay too long and you'll miss your chance!

Don't shoot:

● If the choice is between a really difficult goal attempt and passing to a team-mate in a better position.

● If you are at a very acute angle to the goal (areas shaded here).

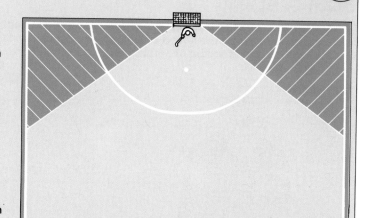

If you are in the areas shaded, it's better to pass to a team-mate.

Where?

You should practise shooting from all angles and to all points of the net. But in a match, some shots are more likely to succeed than others.

● Wherever possible, go for the corner areas highlighted on this diagram — they are the hardest parts of the goal for the goalkeeper to cover.

● Shots from directly in front of the goalkeeper are hardest for him to read because you have a wide choice of angles.

● Shoot diagonally across the goalkeeper if possible.

Goalkeeping

Goalkeeping is a specialist position which deserves a whole book to itself. Good goalkeeping requires a combination of skill, courage, mobility, speed and concentration. It needs a good understanding of 'angles' (see opposite). It also demands a strong voice!

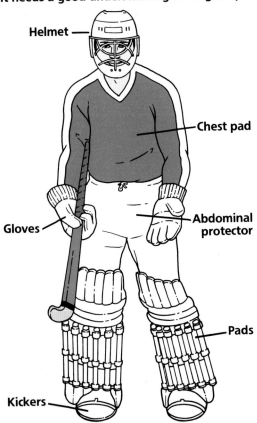

Helmet

Chest pad

Gloves

Abdominal protector

Pads

Kickers

It is essential for a goalkeeper to wear the full range of protective clothing. A helmet with integral facemask is now obligatory.

Functions of the goalkeeper

1. Defending the goal

This is the obvious one!

● You can use any part of your body or your stick to stop the ball, provided you are within the shooting circle, but you must not hold it.

● You must not strike at the ball with your hand or thrust it away with your body — only stop it. You may kick the ball away, however, or use a *save-clear* technique (see page 40).

● Keep your eyes on the game all the time and don't let your concentration slip.

● Use your legs and feet to stop low shots and hands and body for higher ones (see pages 40-41).

● Use your stick only for shots which you cannot otherwise reach.

2. Starting attack

Sometimes you will only be able to deflect the ball over the side lines and out of danger. But if you have time, remember that you are the first line of attack as well as the last line of defence. Try to send the ball to a team-mate who can start up an attack. Using your instep will give your kick most power (see page 40).

3. Organising the defence

Remember that you are in a unique position, facing the game and able to see exactly what is going on.

● Be in control of the circle.

● Use your voice — call, warn and advise your defence players continually.

● Be confident, so team-mates respect your calls.

Understanding the angles

You need to know how to 'narrow the angle' so the attacker has the smallest possible target. Timing is vital and will only come with practice.

1. With the goalkeeper on the line (1) the forward (2) has a wide choice of angles. Move goalie (1) and the angles are much more limited.

2. For shots from the side, imagine lines drawn from both goal posts to the ball and position yourself halfway between them about 3-4yds (2.7-3.6m) away from the goal.

Basic stance

You should adopt this position whenever you are actually in action. From it you are ready to move quickly, up or down and in any direction.

● Legs and back bent, head forward.

● Chin, knees and toes should all be in line.

● Heels off the ground.

● Position of stick and hands can vary according to your own preference, as long as you are able to move quickly when required.

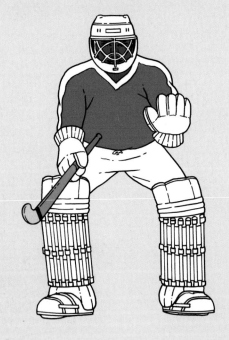

Using your legs

You can either stop the ball and then send it clear with your stick or a kick, or use the *save-clear* technique which does both in one sweeping movement.

The save-clear method is almost always used today. Here you don't stop the ball but use either foot to kick and drive the ball away. Get your head over the ball as you kick, and kick the ball along the ground, not into the air.

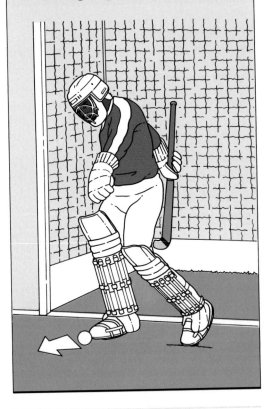

Using your hands and stick

Sometimes you will need to use your hands or stick to save a goal. The principles are the same for both, with the stick really being an extension of your hand. Remember that you must not hold the ball.

● Lead with your head.

● Let your palm or the stick 'give' a little to absorb the impact.

● You can either stop the ball dead or deflect the ball over or round the goal post.

● If you kill the ball so it drops to your feet, quickly clear it with your foot or the stick.

● Keep your eye on the ball all the time.

Diving saves

Obviously, if a shot is out of reach, you will have to dive for it. But don't fall to the ground unless it's absolutely necessary, and always get up and regain your basic stance immediately. The technique for making a diving save is very similar to a soccer goalkeeper.

● Your stick will stay in your right hand, so if you're diving to the right, your left hand comes across for the save.

● For high saves, the rules do allow you to use your stick above shoulder height; in practice, though, it will usually be your left hand that makes the save.

General Tactics

Hockey is a tactical game and outwitting your opponents can be vital to your team's success. Tactics is all about teamwork: individual skill is important, of course, but never forget that you are part of a team.

Planning a match

Good teams use well-rehearsed set pieces, especially when taking free hits, push-ins/hit-ins, long corners, penalty corners and penalty strokes. The team coach or manager decides on the tactics for a game — but the plan often changes or is modified at half-time, depending on how the match is going!

Triangles

Watch the ball as it is played from player to player during a match and you'll see that it's easier to keep possession by passing in a zig-zag pattern than in a straight line. So 'think triangles' and try to position yourself so that you are one point of a three-person triangle supporting and co-operating with each other.

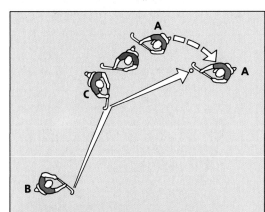

Imagine you are player A. Your team-mate B has passed the ball to C but C can't pass to you because you're marked. By moving as shown, you have made yourself an effective point of a triangle, ready to receive the pass.

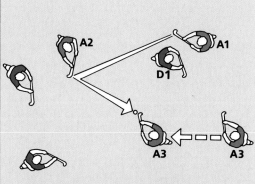

To beat defender D1, A1 passes to A2 positioned at 'point' of triangle. A2 passes to A3 hence beating the defender D1.

Systems of Play

The system adopted for a match is decided by the team manager or coach and will depend on a number of factors including the skills of the players and the known strengths and weaknesses of the opposition. Here are the two most popular systems.

5-3-2-1

So-called because there are five forwards, three midfielders, two backs and one goalkeeper. This is a very popular system, commonly adopted in school and junior club teams. Its main strength lies in its flexibility in defence, with the full backs working closely together and able to change position according to play.

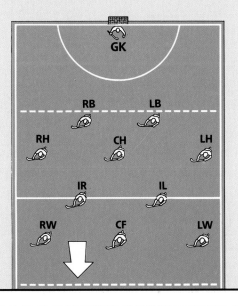

3-3-3-1

Known as a sweeper system because one defender is positioned behind the rest of the defence (other than the goalkeeper of course!) to 'sweep up' through-balls and to cover any unmarked attackers. This system has developed as a variation on the 5-3-2-1, basically replacing the two full backs with the sweeper and a defender who exclusively marks the centre forward. Useful if the opposition's centre forward is particularly dangerous.

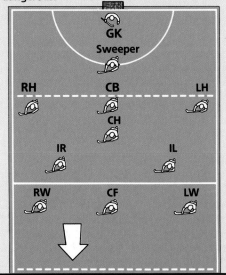

Restarts and Set Plays

Penalty (short) corner

This has become the most important set piece in hockey as it creates many goal scoring opportunities.
Therefore it is important to have a good attacking routine if your team is to score, and just as important is
to have a good defence to prevent the opposition from scoring.

Attacking

It is best to have one routine which is
practised regularly and works. One or two
variations to unsettle the defence should also
be in your armoury.

The ball is hit out from the goal line by an
attacker to a team-mate who stops the ball
'dead' for another attacker to shoot at goal.
The shot, if a hit is used, must be below the
18-inch back board (unless deflected by a
defender). If the shot is a flick the ball can
enter the goal at any height. Other attackers
run towards the goal to 'follow-up' any
rebounds.

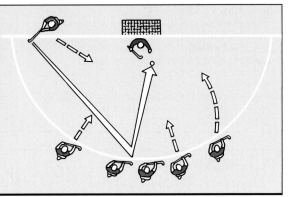

Defending

Only five defenders are allowed behind the
goal line to defend a short corner. The five
defenders usually have the following roles:

No. 1. runner: when the ball is hit in, the
runner speeds towards the ball to block
the shot.

No. 2. runner: runs to a few yards behind
the No. 1 runner to cover any passes made by
the attackers.

Right post: defends the right post.

Left post: defends the left post.

The attackers have an advantage as they will
probably have more players than the
defenders during a short corner.

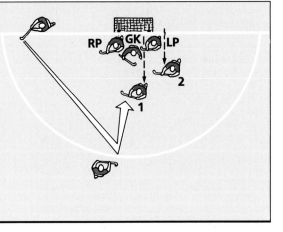

Long corners

The aim is for the attacking side to get the ball into the 'danger zone' (the circle) — so that a shot at goal or a short corner results. Usually the ball is hit into the circle to another attacker's stick. The defending side must try to prevent the ball entering the circle and win possession of the ball.

Hit-ins and free hits

It is unlikely that a long pass will reach its target as too many defenders will be between you and your team-mate. Therefore try to play a short pass to a team-mate (remember the principle of triangles). When defending these two set pieces it is usual to have a ring of players surrounding the ball.

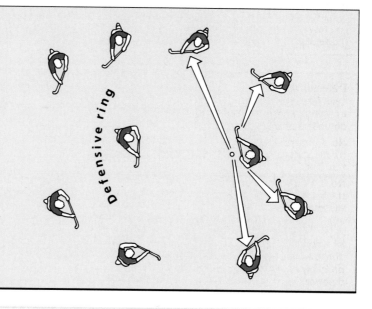

Defensive ring

WARM-UP AND PRACTICE

Fitness

Until adolescence, players do not need any special fitness training — playing the game and practising skills will be enough. But if you are over sixteen or so, your coach will help you devise a fitness programme tailored to your needs.

Warm-up

Warming up with gentle stretching exercises is vital before a match — and advisable as preparation before even an informal game or practice session with friends. If you play without stretching your muscles first, you are more liable to aches the next day and to injuries. Here are some suggestions for your warm-up, which should last at least ten minutes.

1 Arm swings

Make circular movements with your arms, in both directions. Do five for each arm.

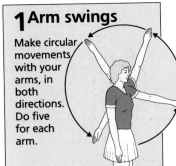

2 Calf and thigh stretches

Kick your legs up behind you, as high as you can. Do the same again, this time holding your leg, as shown.

3 Jogging and sprinting

Run around the pitch at a jogging pace, interspersed with short sprints.

4 Groin and hamstring stretches

Stretch one leg out to the side, the other bent as shown, and hold for a count of five. Do three each side.

5 Back and stomach stretches

Bending from the hips, touch your right foot with your left hand, then straighten up and repeat on the other side. Ten each side.

6 Trunk rotation

Twist your upper body from side to side, keeping your legs and hips facing forward. Repeat eight times.

Practice

You should aim to practise all the techniques described on pages 20-37. Your coach will have some suggestions for games and exercises to improve specific skills — for example, dribbling around a course of cones or other obstacles. But this page gives you some further ideas for practising on your own effectively and enjoyably.

1 Shuttle running

This will improve your speed and agility.
Mark two lines about 10 yds (9.14 m) apart.
Sprint continuously between them, bending to touch the lines at each end.

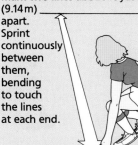

2 Stopping the ball

You can practise this skill using a softer ball such as a tennis ball. Bounce it against a wall at every possible angle and practise getting it under control with your stick.

3 Hit practice

A set of plastic skittles is ideal for practising the hit. Line them up and give yourself a time limit. How many can you knock over in 30 seconds?

4 Flick practice

Mark a wall into numbered zones and try to flick the ball into each one in sequence, without stopping to set up in between. Don't move on to the next zone until you get the previous one right, and try to beat your record each time.

5 Zig-zag hopping

Another footwork improver, and good for strengthening your ankles. Hop on your right foot for 30 yds (27.4 m), then turn round and hop back on your left foot. Drive high, hard and fast.

Glossary

In this glossary you will find explanations of unfamiliar terms encountered in the text together with some you may hear while playing or watching the game.

ADVANTAGE When the umpires allow play to continue even when an offence has been committed. They will do this if stopping play would further disadvantage the team offended against.

BULLY Procedure adopted to restart play after injury or after simultaneous offences committed by members of opposing teams. Previously used to start a game but now replaced with a *passback*.

CHIP A sharply lifting stroke, now illegal.

CIRCLE The shooting circle, actually a semi-circle and also known as the 'D'.

DRIBBLE To move with the ball kept under close control.

FEINT Make fake movements to disguise an intended action.

FLICK A stroke which pushes and lifts a moving or stationary ball.

FREE-HIT Means by which the non-offending team restarts play after an infringement.

GREEN CARD The triangular green card is shown to a player by an umpire as a warning.

HIT-IN Means by which the ball is put back into play from the side-line after leaving the pitch. It is taken by a member of the team which did not put the ball out of play.

INDIAN DRIBBLE A form of *dribble* which originated in India, whereby the ball is tapped forward by repeatedly alternating from right to left with the stick.

INTERCEPT To take possession of the ball while it is being passed from one opponent to another.

MAN-TO-MAN MARKING A system of defence in which each player *marks* a specific member of the opposing team; as opposed to *zonal defence*.

MARK To stay close to an opponent and make it difficult for them to take possession of the ball or get away from you.

OBSTRUCTION This is an offence and occurs when a player interposes any part of his/her body or stick between an opponent and the ball and thereby stops the opponent from playing the ball.

OPEN-SIDE The use of the face of the stick when held on your right side. cf *reverse-side*.

PASSBACK Also referred to as push back. The method of starting the game which replaces the old *bully*.

PUSH-IN see *hit-in*.

RED CARD The circular red card is shown to a player by an umpire to indicate permanent suspension from the game.

REVERSE-SIDE The use of the face of the stick in a reverse position, ie twisted to face backwards.

SAVE-CLEAR A goalkeeping technique which uses the power of a shot to drive the ball away in one movement.

SCANNING Looking up quickly to take in an overall view of the game.

SHORT CORNER Same as a penalty corner (see p15).

16-YARD HIT Free hit to the defenders after the ball has been sent over the back-line by an attacking player. Same as a goal kick in soccer.

SWEEPER A system which uses a single, versatile defender at the back of the field of play.

THIRD-PARTY OBSTRUCTION An offence caused by a player who is not in possession of the ball getting between the ball and an opponent and allowing a team-mate an unfair advantage.

YELLOW CARD The square yellow card is shown to a player by an umpire to indicate temporary suspension from a game.

ZONAL DEFENCE A system of defence in which a player marks any opponents who enter a designated zone of the pitch. As opposed to *man-to-man marking*.

Printed in Italy